RACHEL'S 5 MIRACLES

How a Father's Faith Saw His Daughter through Human Trafficking

Rachel Thomas and Keith Cooper

ISBN 979-8-89043-738-9 (paperback)
ISBN 979-8-89243-077-7 (hardcover)
ISBN 979-8-89043-739-6 (digital)

Copyright © 2024 by Rachel Thomas and Keith Cooper

All rights reserved. No part of this publication may be reproduced, distributed, or transmitted in any form or by any means, including photocopying, recording, or other electronic or mechanical methods without the prior written permission of the publisher. For permission requests, solicit the publisher via the address below.

Christian Faith Publishing
832 Park Avenue
Meadville, PA 16335
www.christianfaithpublishing.com

Printed in the United States of America

Introduction

This is a story about a young woman who fell into a trap—a devious and deadly trap—living in two opposing worlds: one of a middle-class nineteen-year-old college student and the other—a dark, sinister, violent, and evil world. This is a story of a young woman living in hell and the story of how she was eventually snatched out! It's also a love story—a father-daughter story of redemption and restoration. We hope this book encourages you. You might shed a tear. Hopefully, you will also smile and perhaps even laugh.

There are no chapters in this book. Rachel and I take turns sharing our experiences over a period of time. My timeline started in 1984 when Rachel was born. Her timeline starts in 2004 while she was nineteen away at college. The idea for this book came when Rachel showed me a recording of a speech she wrote and delivered at an antitrafficking fundraiser. I had never heard some of the details of Rachel's story of escaping human trafficking, and after nearly eighteen years, it brought back details of my own parallel story as the parent of a child trying to recover from human trafficking. Rachel's speech "My 5 Miracles" is the foundation of what we are sharing in this book. Often, we don't appreciate or even realize our miracles until we stop and look back—look back to see just how we got from there to here.

Rachel, 2004

"You are gorgeous. Has anyone ever told you that you should be a model?"

I took a small step away from my group of friends to hear what this stranger in a nice suit was saying. I was nineteen, a junior at Emory University, enjoying a night out at a popular college hangout. "Uh, yeah," I responded politely. I had heard it before. I've been 5'8" since ninth grade and had been approached by a "model scout" in a mall back in high school with my mom. The scout lavished me with compliments and invited me to an exclusive "model boot camp" to jump-start my career. After begging my parents to pay the exorbitant fees and then receiving a graduation pencil after pretty much just walking with a book on my head for four Saturdays, I knew what my response to this scout was going to be—thanks but no thanks!

"Of course, you have. You've definitely got the looks. My name is Mike. I'm the number 1 modeling agent in Atlanta, and I know talent when I see it." He pulled a business card out of his fitted three-piece suit and held it out with a confident smile. He waved over two young women who were standing nearby and appeared to be around my age. "This is Michelle, one of my models. Michelle just signed a contract with Clinique for $400,000." Michelle smiled meekly and nodded in agreement. I was more impressed by her friendly and humble demeanor than the contract; although she was beautiful, she wasn't stuck up about it. She seemed like someone I could become friends with. I congratulated her and took the card from Mike's hand.

With intense eye contact, Mike continued, "I want to invest in your modeling career if you'll let me. I wanna pay to get you a set of comp cards—it's like a model's resume with a few different looks, height, weight, measurements, things like that—and see how far we can take you. Actually, I guarantee I can get you a paid modeling gig in under a month. And when I do, you can sign with my agency. And, well, if I don't"—he shrugged his shoulders—"I will. There's no way you won't get booked. You've definitely got the looks."

"Okay, thank you," I said as I put the card in my pocket and turned back toward my friends. An agent wanting to invest in me sounded so much better than a scout wanting me to invest in boot camp. *Maybe this time will be better.*

When I called Mike the next day, he was happy to hear from me. "Hey, superstar! I was hoping to hear from you!" He jumped right to business (which I much appreciated). "Michelle actually has a photo shoot already set up for Saturday, and it'd be perfect for you to join."

As he started telling me the address to the studio, I interrupted him, "Whoa, whoa, whoa. I'm not just going to meet you guys at some random studio. (My parents raised me smarter than that!) If I come, I need to bring a friend, maybe two," I announced.

"Okay, Ms. Paranoid," Mike playfully responded. "Bring whoever you want. I'm just glad you're coming. It's gonna be great."

I went to the photo shoot that Saturday with a friend, and I can remember feeling silly that I had been so cautious. Everything seemed legit—professional photographers, bright lights, hanging backdrops, racks of clothing, tables of accessories, hair and makeup artists, the whole nine. And there was Michelle confidently striking poses. This was already running laps around that boot camp scam.

Two weeks later, Mike kept his promise. He landed me a paid modeling gig in a music video for a Grammy Award–winning artist—another cool experience. But this time, in addition to photographers, lighting, and hair and makeup, there were celebrities there and free food! It all felt like a big party.

"Great job today, superstar." Mike came up to me at the end of the shoot and told me that in order to receive payment, I needed to fill out a W-9. Having worked at the YWCA before, I knew what that was—that simple tax form you fill out in order to be paid. I completed it right there on set with my full name, my permanent address (which is my parents' home address back in Pasadena), my current address (where I was living with my roommate near campus in Atlanta), my social security number, and my signature.

I handed the W-9 to Mike, assuming he would hand it to the casting director, and I would receive a check in the mail. I didn't even think twice about it.

Fast forward to another two weeks, Mike invited me to attend my first "industry mixer." He described it as an invitation-only event where "who's who" from the entertainment industry get together to network. I met him and Michelle around 8:00 p.m. at a restaurant parking lot so I could leave my car. Apparently, there was a "tight guest list," and they would only valet one car per party. I got in Mike's BWM 745, and we were off. Michelle was driving, Mike was in the front seat typing away on his phone, and I was in the back seat, buckled up for another cool adventure.

About twenty minutes into our ride, a song came on the radio. "Hey, I like this. Who sings this?" Mike asked while casually bobbing to the music. A moment of silence went by as I expected Michelle to respond.

I leaned up from the back seat and projected over the music. "It's Maxwell. It's called 'Lifetime.'"

Mike peered at Michelle and became instantly enraged. He reached over and slapped Michelle so hard that her head hit the window. "B——, don't you ever f——ing ignore me!" He hit her again. "You wanna f——ing ignore me!" He kept his hand open, but the blows were heavy, the palm of his hand landing squarely on her face. "You think that's funny?" With wild rage in his face, he was now sitting near the edge of the seat with his whole body turned toward hers.

"Mike, no, I'm so sorry. I'm so sorry, I didn't hear you. I didn't hear you." Michelle had one hand on the steering wheel and one hand instinctively yet weakly raised to her face. He kept yelling, and she kept apologizing. No tears, no look of shock or surprise, just repeated apologies while trying to secure eye contact with Mike and steal glances at the road. It was like she wanted him to see the sincerity on her face. Like when Beauty grabbed the beast's face and make him stare into her eyes to calm down.

Mike finally stopped yelling, but he kept his arm cocked in the air. He was glaring at Michelle and breathing with his whole chest. The way he stared at her was like a bully, weighing if his victim was fully submissive or if he needed to give one more blow to finish her off. He flinched toward her and the car jerked to the left. I don't know if it was the sudden jerk, the eye contact, or bully satisfaction, but Mike quickly deflated—his chest went back to normal, his eyebrows unfurled. He sunk back into his seat and got back on his phone. With the episode now over, Michelle adjusted in her seat, wiped the hair out of her face, put two hands on the wheel, and kept on driving.

I had never seen abuse before. I had never seen a man that angry before. I wanted to cry. I wanted to sob. I wanted to pull over, get out, and go home. But I sat there, frozen. We drove another few minutes, and then we were at the mixer. Autopilot must have kicked in because I was able to go in there with them and actually function. I shook people's hands. I said thank-yous to compliments. I smiled back when people smiled at me (even including Mike), but inside my mind was racing. *They're way more than model and agent. They must be boyfriend and girlfriend. He's one of those abusive boyfriends my mom warned me about. Poor Michelle. Why would she be with him? She really needs to break up with him, and I need to get away too.*

When I finally made it back home that night, I couldn't sleep. I kept thinking of ways to try to help Michelle get out of her abusive relationship. I just couldn't understand why she would be with him. She was so pretty, and he was like fifteen years older than us. Maybe she loved him. Sad.

The next morning, in my sweetest voice, I called Mike. "You know what, finals are coming up soon, and it's getting really hard for me to juggle modeling and school. I need to take a break for now to focus on school, but I'll definitely call you when I'm ready to pick back up."

Silence.

"Hello? Mike, are you there?"

In a low, serious tone I heard, "B———, I own you. You're gonna do what I tell you to do, or somebody's gonna get hurt." I heard him ruffle some papers. "Three, seven, one, two, Birchwood Lane, Pasadena, CA, 91012." My parents' address. He told me when and where to meet him that night and said if I don't come to him, he's coming to me. He read my address there in Atlanta and then hung up.

I remember standing in my living room and the room just fading to black, like in the movies. *What. Just. Happened.* My heart was pounding. *What should I do? Did he just threaten me? Should I call the police? Do police respond to threats? If I tell the police I saw him hit Michelle, can I start a case on her behalf? Should I call my parents? Should I tell my best friend? What's happening right now? Why is he doing this?* After playing through several scenarios in my head, I forced myself not to overreact. *Mike's been a cool guy for the past month, and I did just sign that contract. He did flip out on his girlfriend last night, but they recovered, I guess. They seem used to that. He's never yelled at me or hurt me. He has no reason to. Let me just stay on his good side and smooth things over so I can make a smoother exit later.*

I showed up when and where Mike told me to meet him that night, and he had a buyer waiting for me in the back seat of his car. When he met me in the parking lot and told me what he expected me to do, I started crying. "Mike, please do not make me do this. Please don't."

He grabbed my arm very tightly and said, "You're gonna do what I tell you to do. Don't make me hurt you."

After I was raped in the back seat, the buyer got out and left. Mike got in the front seat and locked the doors. He turned all the way around to look me squarely in my wet eyes. "If you call the police"—he didn't blink at all—"if you tell anyone, I will kill your parents, and then I will kill you."

Never before had I been so traumatized. Never before had I met anyone with such capacity for evil. The darkness of that night and the gravity of those words sunk in deep. I believed him. That was the first night I was thrown into the pit of human trafficking.

Dad, 1984 to 2004

It seems as if Rachel (our second daughter and last of two children) was born with a smile on her face. When I picture her in my mind, she is always smiling. She was a sweet girl, a girly girl, who had special dolls she loved. As she grew, she was kind, generous, and thoughtful. She was friendly and would often share that she had made a new friend at school or wherever she was that day. She always loved to laugh, and she was inclusive, trying to bring everyone into whatever was happening. Rachel was a good student, and it seemed like it came easy to her. She won spelling bees in elementary school. She was popular and funny.

At times, Rachel had trouble going to sleep. Everyone else in the house would be asleep, and I would check on her. We would just smile at each other. A few times, late at night, she would get scared and not be able to sleep. She would come to my side of the bed and wake me. I would get out of bed and let her lay down there next to my wife; I would go and sleep on the floor. We will never forget that Halloween when Rachel really wanted a full ET costume. As she was in it, she just seemed to channel the receptive, gentle spirit of ET, and the little kids kept saying, "ET. ET" as they wanted to hug her and touch her finger.

She was so kindhearted, very considerate of others, a joy to be around, and one who could cheer you up. For the most part, she was a team player. However, she did have a competitive side that came out when she played Scrabble. My wife, Marlene, was also pretty competitive on the Scrabble board; they were both good players and played each other hard. My wife purchased a book on how to improve your Scrabble game. The book contained a list of unusual but acceptable two- and three-letter words. When my wife realized that Rachel had memorized all those words before she could even get a good look at them, she got a little upset. Truth be told, I would catch them playing at night with sunglasses on. They both claimed the other one would try to see where they were thinking about playing next and would play there just out of spite. It reminded me of the "Spy vs. Spy" section in the quirky comic book, *Mad* magazine, where the two opposing spies would run around, always in sunglasses, trying to do serious damage to one another!

Rachel was quick to sincerely ask for your advice concerning a matter, showing her humility and respect for other's advice; she was a people person.

After going to a private middle school, Rachel wanted to go to the local public high school instead of a private school, and we hesitantly agreed. She promised us she would work hard and do well. She made working hard look easy—I never saw her sweating about any schoolwork. She was a pretty good writer and could put out a ten-page report/paper effortlessly the night before it was due (she was a night owl). I don't remember her having any difficult academic challenges.

In her junior year, I went to her back-to-school night, going from classroom to classroom, meeting her teachers. As I was walking into one of her classrooms, the teacher looked up at me, and she immediately burst out with, "Oh, you must be high maintenance's father." I looked to see if I still had my work ID card on, but I didn't. How did the teacher figure out I was her father? And why was she referring to Rachel like that? I had never really thought of Rachel as high maintenance. Now, some say I spoiled my daughters, and then some say they came here spoiled, and I was just "working" my part, doing my job.

Rachel played sports as a youth. By the time she was in the ninth grade, Rachel, the youngest in the house, was now the tallest one in the house. She was blessed with an athletic build. She played on her high school volleyball team and was a pitcher on the softball team.

When I was working, I looked forward to and enjoyed going to both of my daughters' (Kristin and Rachel) junior high and high school softball, volleyball, and basketball games. I was so blessed to be able to attend most of their games! In fact, I will never forget the time I went to one of Rachel's seventh-grade softball games. The umpire canceled at the last minute, so they asked me to call the game, or there would be no game. I was the only spectator there. So trying to be Mr. "nice guy," I agreed. And there I was in a county park at

4:00 p.m. in my business attire, trying to squeeze my big head into a girl catcher's face mask, hoping and praying the whole time that my work pager wouldn't go off! But the worst of it was having to call Rachel "out" for looking at strike three at least once and her team lost the game.

I tucked Rachel and her sister in and said prayers with them most nights from the time they were about two years old until they were about eleven. When Rachel was seven years old, she joined the youth choir at our church and sang in our church's choirs until she graduated from high school. Her high school best friend was our pastor's daughter. As her high school Sunday school teacher at our church, she and I would often have discussions concerning various biblical subjects.

Rachel worked for the YWCA for a couple of summers while in high school. She loved that job and received several accolades for the work she did. She excelled in high school and graduated among the top ten students in her class. Rachel and her mother visited several of the colleges that had accepted Rachel, and she decided to go to Emory University in Atlanta, Georgia. Even while she was at Emory, we talked about once a week. Sometimes, she would have a question concerning a biblical verse or a biblical principle. Often, one of her girlfriends would be conferenced in with us. Rachel worked as an RA (residential advisor) at Emory and sang in an acapella group during her freshman and sophomore years.

Rachel, 2005

After the first night I was trafficked, there were many more. My story isn't like *Taken* or the many other movies that portray trafficking where a girl is kidnapped, drugged, tied up, and held in a shipping container or motel room. I lived in my apartment. For the first few months, I attended classes. I talked to my parents once or twice a week, though I only answered or returned their calls when I was able to put on a convincingly happy voice. I isolated myself from my friends by telling them I was "going through something" and needed space. I bared down and did my best to survive, not knowing the depths of the world I had been ushered into.

Mike's rule was that I be available to him whenever he called. If I didn't answer by the second ring, day or night, there would be a punishment. And, when I wasn't with him, I had to work at a strip club six days a week and give him money. Sometimes, he would come to the strip club and arrange "dates" for me after my shift was over. Sometimes, he would bring us (he had about six to ten girls at any given time) to nightclubs, sporting events, and music festivals to sell us. He was, in fact, very well connected in the entertainment industry in Atlanta, so many celebrities, athletes, and men of status had his number and would call him to supply the "model style" girls for their parties or personal use. We were sometimes even sold to uniformed police officers who appeared to be Mike's friends. He prided himself on being the "multicultural modeling agent" with girls of every race. We also did some legitimate music video and magazine modeling that Mike booked through his connections with entertainment industry executives. It all built his credibility, padded his pockets, and made it easier for him to trap victims. He was a nice, fun guy in public and pure evil behind closed doors.

Every time I found some courage to resist or plead with Mike, I would get hit so hard that I became disoriented. As "models," we weren't allowed to look beat up, so whenever he hit us, it was in our head where our hair would cover any lumps or bruises.

But honestly, human trafficking isn't only about violence and threats and physical and sexual abuse. It's the mental, emotional, and spiritual manipulation that really create the invisible chain around the brain that robs victims of their self-worth and true identity.

One night, we were at a popular college hangout, and Mike spotted a girl he wanted. By that time, I had appeared in four music videos and a local magazine, so Mike was using me as his poster child. He told me to go introduce myself to her and tell her that she should meet my agent. I went up to her and tapped her on the shoulder. When she turned around, she looked just like my little cousin with dimples and freckles. She looked so young and so innocent. I looked her in the eyes and said, "Turn around and walk away. Just turn around and walk away." She looked at me in confusion for a moment and then her eyes shifted slightly to the right to look past me. "Hey, beauties, what's going on here?" Mike said with a smile.

"Umm...I don't know. She just told me to turn around and walk away," the girl replied.

Mike pinched my lower back so hard that my eyes began to water. "She's always playing around like that. I'm Mike. I'm the number one modeling agent in Atlanta, and you are *gorgeous*!" He started his pitch, but she kept looking at my face, and thank God she walked away. The punishment I got later that night made me lose my will to put my moral compass above my survival.

I'm not sure it was a conscious decision, but I know that from that day forward, I never purposely foiled another recruiting assignment. That became one of my regular assignments—a recruiting quota of at least two numbers every night we went out. I never thought I would face charges for bringing girls to meet my "agent," but there's never a way to anticipate or control just how deep and low the bottom can go while you're falling in a pit.

Almost a year into being trafficked, I got a call from the Atlanta Police Department. "Rachel, you have been named as an accomplice to a trafficker. You can come in and tell us what happened, or we can put a warrant out for your arrest and come get you."

I was shaking as I drove to the Atlanta Police Station. Mike's threats resounded even louder now that I had seen his capacity for violence.

At the station, I was interrogated for hours by two officers who were cold, accusatory, and belittling. Even while sitting in a police station, it felt safer to stay on Mike's good side than to trust these officers to help me. After hours of silence, they got frustrated and left.

When the door reopened, it was a different guy. He stepped in and noticed that I was freezing. "Are you cold? Do you want something to drink?" He left for a moment and came back with an oversized sweatshirt and a bottle of water.

As he leaned down to place the water, we made eye contact.

"Wow, you remind me of my daughter."

Miracle number 1—one moment of compassion and connection from one officer overrode a slew of bad experiences with multiple officers and instantly changed my ability to trust in a system that had let me down.

It would be Detective J. T. Summers I would feel safe enough to tell my story to. It would be Detective J. T. Summers who would tell me I was a victim and that it wasn't my fault. Even when I told him about my recruiting quota and how many girls I helped Mike recruit, he told me I could be a hero for ten times as many by bringing Mike down. He was in the room when I made calls on a recorded line. J. T. Summers was in the room when Mike told me I sounded weird and that he was headed to my house for a private conversation. It was J. T. Summers who would park outside my friend's apartment and sleep there, answer my phone calls day or night, and make me feel genuinely protected enough, long enough to stay and testify to the grand jury. Then it became too dangerous for me to stay, so I had to go. I called my parents two weeks into what was supposed to be my senior year. "Mom, Dad, can you pick me up tonight from the airport?" They were shocked. "What? Why! Girl, you better not be pregnant!"

"I'll tell you when I see you. Please just be there tonight." It was the longest, most silent, most awkward ride home from the airport and the most tension I had ever felt around our kitchen table. "Rachel, you gotta tell us something," my dad broke the silence. I achingly began the story of how I met a man who told me that I was beautiful and that he would be my modeling agent, and then he turned crazy and forced me to have sex with people and that he has their home address and that the police haven't arrested him yet, and I dropped out of school and… My words trailed into silence as I saw the slump in their shoulders and the pain in their faces.

"Did he ever hit you?" my dad asked with tears in his eyes.

I thought about the countless times he hit me in my head. I thought about the times he choked me. I thought about the time he beat Denise unconscious in the parking lot and then hit me for crying for her because it showed disloyalty to him. I looked at my dad's face and realized it was too much. "No, he never hit me," I said softly.

I couldn't look at them anymore, and I couldn't tell them anymore. "I'm sorry, I'm really tired, and I just want to go to bed." As I stood up, I accidentally looked at my mom sitting across from me. Her eyes were closed tight, but tears were somehow still falling. I made sure not to look at my dad as I respectfully pushed the chair in and went to my room.

That night, I sat on my bed and wrote out my suicide letter. It was an apology for the wonderful upbringing they had given me and the huge mess I had made. I asked them to tell the rest of the family I loved them and that I was sorry. It was all too much. My plan was to go to the park the next day and take my life—to keep everyone else safe, end my pain, and just take out the trash.

I didn't learn this until much later, but as I was up planning to die, my father was up all night, praying for how to bring me back to life.

Dad, September 30, 2005

The first night, "Lord, Lord, Lord!"

I still vividly remember that day Rachel told us she was coming home from college. When Rachel called to say that she was coming home that night but couldn't give us an explanation, my heart, soul, and mind were shaken! What was going on? How bad is it? *Don't jump to conclusions or make the wrong assumptions*, I told myself. How would we react once she shared the facts with us? What was going to happen next? Would my wife be able to handle it? On and on, all afternoon and into the evening, I was consumed with anxiety.

I prayed for peace and wisdom and for each one of us. My wife and I picked Rachel up from the airport that night, but she would not share anything until after we got home. More agony, wondering, "What was it?" When we finally sat down at the kitchen table, my heart was racing, my mind was exhausted, and my spirit was restless. I could tell that this was very difficult for her. I just kept on praying in my heart and spirit for all three of us, *Lord, have mercy!* Rachel wouldn't tell us what had happened to her until after dinner. Finally, she broke through her tears and was able to reveal her secret life to us.

Oh, God! I can't believe this. What, why, why? I said internally. Our world was rocked. It was too much for us to comprehend even partially! We talked, cried, and/or sat in silence until we decided to go to bed. My wife and I met in our bedroom. We just hugged each other and agreed to get some rest and deal with everything in the morning. I think it was around 10:30 p.m. or 11:00 p.m., close to our normal bedtime. I laid down, but there was no rest for me. My mind was lit, on fire with words, thoughts, and questions all on top of each other, dueling for attention! Guilt, depression, unbelief, grief, shame, humiliation, anger, hurt, and self-pity. That was a very long night for me. There were so many, many issues, questions, and hurts bombarding my heart and mind! How could this happen? Why did it happen to Rachel, to us? Why didn't she come to us sooner? How could she endure so much abuse and violence? How could we talk weekly, and I couldn't read between the lines?

I was hurting, crying, confused, and overwhelmed with shame, guilt, disbelief, anger, and feeling like a failure! Rachel, who is so kind, sweet, trusting, and considerate. I started to weep again. What should I have done better? Why is all of this happening? Was this all my fault? My wife had said maybe we should send our daughters to the local city college until they mature some. But I insisted that they experience the four-year college life. Why didn't I listen to her? Why didn't I pursue some of my strange feelings I had at times when Rachel and I talked? Rachel and I could talk for an hour at a time. Why was I so blind? Who else knew about this? Why did she have to go through all of this—the abuse, fear, embarrassment, and shame? How did she stay in school? How extremely painful all of this must be to her, to have this kind of past and to face us and her future.

I kept coming back around to why, why us, how did she get so caught up? What did I do wrong? Hours went by, and I couldn't let it go. It was past 2:00 a.m., and my mind was still going around in circles, spiraling down deeper into despair! Finally, being so exhausted, I just asked God to help me, tell me what to do, and speak to me. He said, "This is a test of the unconditional love that you have professed to Rachel. You can focus on your pain and issues, or you can focus on her pain and needs at this time. If you do love her unconditionally, you must convey that to Rachel and show her by focusing on her needs right now! Let go of all of your questions about the past year. The important issue now is Rachel's mental state of mind and her recovery! That is the race which has been set before you (Hebrews 12:1), demonstrating, working out your unconditional love for Rachel. Rachel's recovery is your goal and focus!"

I was so happy and excited to have been given my direction—my first step on this journey! I could hardly wait for the morning to come so I could share with Rachel my love for her! Weeping endured that night, but praise God joy came in the morning! "Weeping may endure for a night, but joy cometh in the morning" (Psalm 30:5).

Rachel, October 1, 2005

The next morning, as soon as I stepped out of my bedroom, they were waiting. They had cooked breakfast and were sitting around the kitchen table again. We sat in silence for a while. Then my dad asked me to stand up. He came and put his arms around me, and then my mom joined in.

He said, "Rachel, we don't know what you've done. We don't know what you've been through, but we know there is nothing so bad you could ever do that we don't still love you, and that God doesn't still love you."

That was miracle number two. My parents—people who had never heard of human trafficking, who had absolutely no training, no background in social work, no background in therapy, no rule book, no best practices to follow—my parents covered me in exactly the ways I needed in order to begin healing from human trafficking. They didn't pursue the "whys" or the ugly details. They couldn't give me a trained listening ear or specialized services, but they gave me grace and made sure my tangible needs were met. Thank God for people who don't kick you when you're down.

Dad, October 1, 2005

It was the second day and night. *Help me, Jesus!*

By the end of the day, I was beginning to find myself full of anger, hating the man responsible for all of this. I felt violated from hearing just the little bit of Rachel's ordeal she had shared with us, knowing she had sheltered us from many of the ugly realities she had endured. I wanted to do something to him, to punish him, and to avenge Rachel. How could I just let it go and wait to see if justice would take place? I felt my manhood challenged. That evening, I was emotionally tormented. "God, how can I just do nothing? Help me"

"Look at you, with your Sunday school teaching, choir singing, deacon self, now, what exactly are you going to do? Who are you going to call?" For a moment there, I didn't know if those were my words, the Holy Spirit, or another spirit speaking. I fantasized about bad things happening to him. But then, after a while, reality set in. What was I going to actually do? I already knew what God was going to tell me to do, but I didn't want to hear it. Just let me linger in my disgust of him and the evilness of this world for a while. I didn't want to surrender my will to God just yet. I wanted to hold onto that hate a little longer. I was enjoying hating him, and I felt like I was doing something.

Laying in the bed full of hate and anger, God said, "You are enjoying yourself, aren't you? How long do you plan on relishing in this hate party? The sooner you let it go and forget about it, the better. Do you want to carry this burden around for the next five, ten, or fifteen years? Start the forgiving process now! I am offering you the grace, the power to do just that right now—right now! 'For vengeance is mine, I will repay,' thus saith the Lord (Romans 12:19–21)." Thank God that, by His grace, I was able to lay that burden down!

Dad, October 2 to November 10, 2005

Rachel was home two days before she started looking for an apartment to move to in a city two hours away from our home. She and I would take trips to that city, trying to find the right place. A week later, I moved her into a small apartment she would share with other college women. Rachel didn't like being alone; she likes being with people. As we finished moving her clothes in there, I turned to the left then I looked to the right, then I said, "Rachel, where are you going to sleep?"

Immediately the Spirit said, "Shut up, let it go." So I gave Rachel a big hug, got in my car, and began the two-hour trip home.

As I drove, it all started to come down on me. I started dwelling on the fact that she could have stayed home and finished her undergrad work online. I figured she wanted to get away to clear her head and that she was literally terrified of that man! I began to feel like a failure. I couldn't rescue her, avenge her, nor protect her in my own house. I felt so bad for all of us. How was all of this going to work out? How long would she be there? I felt like I wasn't doing enough. What else should I be doing?

Then the Spirit told me, "Your job is to steadfastly love her unconditionally, be there for her, and support her. It's my job to rescue, redeem, restore, avenge, and protect her. That's my job."

I felt a lot better as if I really did have some worth or value and that I was doing what I was supposed to be doing.

It was dark now. I still had at least an hour left on my trip home. I felt good about the place Rachel had chosen. I thought Rachel would be safe there. She would be with other college girls and be comfortable there. But then fear attacked me. "What about your safety?" Rachel really thought that man could be dangerous! She quickly made her plans, and she hurried up and got out of dodge. He is a very violent man, and he told Rachel he would kill us! And he knows exactly where we live! What if he does try to hurt us? Should I get some guns and move out of the house for a while? Maybe just move and change our names. I really didn't know what that man was capable of. *Lord, have mercy.*

I drove along, trying not to dwell on negative, fearful thoughts but instead praying for direction. I tried hard to stay in a mind of prayer, which enabled me to hold off fear, pushing it back off me. But I needed some help. While waiting on my help, I heard, "You have done what I told you to do, to embrace, and to continue to love Rachel unconditionally, and you forgave that man as much as you can at that point in time. Fear not! It's not your destiny to be tiptoeing around, peeping around corners, changing this and that, and going through all those changes. Fear not. Be at peace, be still." I felt so much better, as if a burden had been lifted off of me!

By the time I got home, I was exhausted; it had been a long day. I was emotionally drained but at peace, for I had gotten my joy back. "For the joy of the Lord is your strength" (Nehemiah 8:10).

Two years before Rachel came home from Emory, I was laid off from my job. I had worked as a manager in a major corporation for twenty-six years. It was hard, but God had prepared me. He told me that I had happily evaded the last few layoff announcements, but my time had come. It was time for me to go.

"Are you sure, Lord? I mean, my wife just retired, and my daughters are still in college."

The response was, "This one has got your name on it. You have got to go." But He didn't tell me where I was going! For whatever reason(s), when Rachel came home from college (two years later), I still didn't have a job. But I was ready, spiritually, emotionally, and physically for Rachel!

A month after Rachel returned home, my wife said, "That's why God laid you off and gave you time—time so you could save Rachel."

Rachel, Winter 2005

I barely left that apartment, primarily because I felt traumatized and depressed; secondarily because I was scared. My dad would come visit periodically and bring me loads of Costco goods. One day in November, I got a call from my academic advisor at Emory

University, inviting me to get back in school. My parents had asked Detective Summers to get a letter from the FBI saying that I was a witness to a crime. They gave the letter to the dean and asked for a favor. For the first time in Emory University's history, they created a distance learning program just for me—miracle number 3.

As soon as I got in touch with one of my passions, my God-given talents, I felt something worthwhile to throw myself into and live for. I've loved learning since before I knew what learning was, and my ultimate career dream had always been to be a teacher and one day open a school. Getting back to school and writing was life-giving for me. For others, it could be art, cooking, fashion design, math, caring for animals, photography, or so many other things. Sparking a passion, feeling like you're good at something, learning a new skill—that's the stuff that purpose and meaning are made of.

While I was rebuilding myself, a team of bold and pioneering heroes were busy forging uncharted territory, building a case. The 2005 reauthorization of the Trafficking Victims Protection Act allowed funding and training for local law enforcement agencies to establish human trafficking units to protect domestic victims.

It was summer of 2005 that a victim reported Mike and me, her recruiter, to the Atlanta Police Department. It had just been in the spring of 2005 that the Atlanta Police Department had established a human trafficking unit. They pulled officers from homicide, narcotics, and vice and told them about a 'new crime' to look out for called human trafficking. When they got the call, they were ready. They acted quickly and brought in the FBI when they learned that Mike had taken us to multiple states. After he was arrested, Mike's name and face was posted on the six o'clock *Atlanta News*. The news anchor implored, "If you have any information or have had any interactions with this man, call the hotline number." They had over seventy-five phone calls in the first hour.

Mike's trafficking dated back seven years. He preyed only on naive college girls who were away from home, promising them glamorous modeling careers. Of all the victims, four of us agreed to testify in the trial. I had no idea, but our case was the first case prosecuted in the nation involving adult victims of sex trafficking. I call that a miracle—miracle number 4. The miracle is that the exact legislation and funding would pass in the exact year that I had a way out and desperately needed the law on my side. Mike's defense was that we all did everything because we wanted to. He said we all asked him to help us sleep our way to the top of a modeling career, and he was simply facilitating our requests. He denied violence. He denied coercion. He denied force. It was his word against ours, and he had music videos and magazines of us looking glamorous and smiling to "prove" that we weren't victims. According to him, we were all adult college students over eighteen doing everything because we wanted to.

It was a daunting job for the entire team led by Civil Rights Division Attorney Karima Maloney and the Assistant US Attorney Susan Coppedge. They had to be bold, creative, diligent, and fearless to see the case through. In the end, Mike went to prison, and I was able to rest a little easier at night.

Dad, 2006 to 2011

Rachel never did move back home. She earned her bachelor's degree from Emory University. We joyfully went to her graduation. I was so grateful for the deans and professors at Emory who made it possible for Rachel to complete her college education.

My wife and I decided to not go to Rachel's trial in Atlanta in 2007. We couldn't see any benefit or blessings in doing so. However, our oldest daughter, Kristin, did go to the trial. She was there to testify if needed to. She would testify that Rachel had called her at times saying she was so afraid that someone named Mike was going to seriously hurt or maybe even kill her.

It wasn't long before Rachel decided she wanted to get a master's degree in education. I went with her to the informational meeting at UCLA. About ten minutes into the meeting, I thought to myself, *I sure am glad that Rachel is going to be doing all of this stuff and not me!* Then I remembered why I didn't pursue grad school, just too many academic hurdles to get into and to complete the degree. However, Rachel seemed totally unfazed and was even cheerfully confident.

Fortunately for Rachel, she had inherited her mother's brains, work ethic, and determination!

Living with three beautiful females (a wife and two daughters), all of whom are much smarter than I am, has its challenges ("help me, Lord") and its rewards ("thank ya, Lord!").

After Rachel earned a master's degree in education from UCLA, she decided to teach. In an effort to have a career that would have a meaningful impact on disadvantaged children, she became a teacher at a public high school in the inner city of one of America's largest cities. She taught English, was the volleyball coach, and mentored students there. It was a typical inner-city high school, with shortages, gangs, drugs, apathy, hopelessness, etc. We helped her decorate her classroom and donated materials.

In her third year there, I enjoyed going to Coach Rachel's volleyball games. It was just like the good old days when I enjoyed going to one of her or her sister's games. It was at one of those volleyball games—an away game—after the game was over. She approached me and she said, "Dad, can we talk?"

I said "Yes, let's go to my car."

I sat in the driver seat, and she got in the backseat on the passenger side and starting crying, "I can't do this anymore."

Rachel, 2011 to Today

When I was a high school teacher, I started seeing my students being preyed upon by the same type of manipulator as Mike. When one of my tenth grade students went missing two weeks after meeting her new boyfriend—who I later learned was in his thirties—it crushed me. I had seen the warning signs, but I didn't intervene. Then she was gone.

Some things break your heart but fix your vision.

I realized I had more to give my students than an English curriculum. I had never shared my story before. I had swept it under the rug, ashamed and embarrassed, but I had a nagging sense that I wasn't living my fullest purpose.

I started googling human trafficking conferences and snuck into a local conference. I heard a woman named Carissa Phelps. She had been a runaway homeless youth and, while living on the streets, met a pimp named Icy who trafficked her. Our stories were very different, but I felt a connection to her. I went up to her after the session to buy her book. She was signing autographs. "Who should I make it out to?"

"My name's Rachel."

"Hi, Rachel. Who are you here with?"

"Nobody. I'm by myself. I'm just here to learn. I think I've been through some of the stuff you were talking about."

"You're a survivor."

It was the first time I'd ever been called that. I didn't even know how to respond. She looked me in my eyes. "Well, Rachel, you're not by yourself anymore." She scooted the book over, pulled out a checkbook, scribbled something down, and then handed me a check for $75. She said, "Everybody here is with an organization that's paying them to be here and to learn how to be part of the solution. We need your voice. We need you here."

I looked at the check, confused, and looked at her. "No, no, I'm not here to speak or anything."

"I know," she said. "But you belong here. You can be with us." She pointed to three other women sitting in the front row—other survivors.

And just like that, I was valued, seen, and included—miracle number 5. I found one person who became the open door to a community I never knew existed and to an impact greater than I could have imagined.

Survivors are some of the strongest, brightest, most passionate, and most inspiring people on the planet. Hardships really have a way of preparing ordinary people for extraordinary destiny. Now, over a decade later, I am still a grateful member of the survivor community, paying forward what was given to me. I've used my passion as an educator to found Sowers Education Group, where we are sowing seeds of awareness and survivor empowerment. We have employed over thirty survivors with meaningful paid opportunities to make a difference. We created the "Ending the Game" curriculum, which is now being used in over three hundred facilities across forty-six states and three countries. It was published in the *Journal of Women in Criminal Justice* and has thousands of graduates to date. Recently, we created The Cool Aunt Series, a human trafficking prevention curriculum for teens, and have partnered with the state of California to bring this series to fifty thousand foster youth.

In 2020, I became a presidential appointee to the United States Advisory Council on Human Trafficking. The council's mandate is to meet with twenty-six different government departments to create solutions to human trafficking together. These are things I didn't even dream big enough to imagine. And I know God's not done with me yet.

I get so overwhelmed with gratitude for the life I'm blessed to live because of the blessings of others. I don't take for granted that I made it to this chapter of my life. And it's not because I'm any better or smarter or more deserving. It's because multiple people showed up for me and did their part well. They didn't know each other, but each miracle became a thread that spread and wove together a strong safety net for me.

Of the other three women who were part of the case with me, one committed suicide, one went back to "the life" and got deep into drugs, and the other said she was going to move away, disappear, and asked us never to reach out to her again.

I wish more people would have shown up for them and that they had safety nets to hold on to. If you are one of the people who show up, thank you. I hope you know who you are. The ironic part is that whenever I call one of my miracle workers a hero, they all say, "No, no, I was just doing my part."

Every person in this fight is part of the thread in the net, making it stronger, wider, more miraculous. I dare you to envision a world where human trafficking is not business as usual. I dare you to believe in the value and resilience of people who are getting ready to turn their biggest setback into an even bigger comeback. I dare you to take ownership of the miracle-working power inside of you. What thread do you bring? Today is the day to show up. And the most beautiful thing about showing up is that as you do your part to strengthen the net, you are uplifted too.

Dad, Today

I am remiss for not thanking God for Rachel's victories every time I see her! Rachel's business and ministry has grown. She travels across the country, teaching, training, and speaking. She tries to hire survivors to fill her staffing needs. She still gets calls at all hours of the day and night—a girl, a teenage girl, or a young woman in desperate need of help!

I remember one Thanksgiving, around 8:00 p.m., Rachel got one of "those" calls. I drove her to a house, watched her go into the house. Was she just going to talk to a girl? Was there anyone else in the house? Would this be an attempted rescue? All I could do was just sit there and stay, prayed up until she got back into my car. She is still getting and taking "those" calls.

Over the first five years of Rachel's recovery, she made five CDs for me. They were all gospel songs about God's forgiveness, redemption, providence, love, and faithfulness. They were therapeutic and a blessing to me. I would listen to them in my quiet time and still do. However, there was one track that was not strictly a gospel song. Rachel made it the first track on the last CD she made for me. It was a song by Beyonce, "My Daddy." Some of the lyrics are:

> Because you loved me I overcome
> You've given me such security
> No matter what mistakes I make you're there for me
> You cure my disappointments and you heal my pain
> That's why I want my unborn son to be like my daddy.

I still tear up every time I hear it! And I'm still amazed and so blessed that about nine years later, Rachel and her husband at the time, Lawrence, gave natural birth to their only child—a boy—on my birthday!

Rachel is just as comfortable counseling/teaching victims, training social workers, or speaking in front of hundreds of well-heeled, well-meaning concerned people. After her speeches, she always receives lots of comments and questions. She told us one comment that really blessed her: "You are more than a conqueror." The woman went on to say, "Not only did you conquer your devil, but you made inroads into his territory, making you more than a conqueror" (Romans 8:37).

Another one of Rachel's favorites was when a woman commented, "I don't know your parents, but I love them."

Rachel was featured in a segment of a CNN special, "Anyone's Daughter" and has been featured in many media outlets including feature films "Wake Up!" and "California's Forgotten Children."

During the Trump administration, Rachel was appointed to the United States Advisory Council on Human Trafficking. The Biden administration reappointed her to the Council. She is so blessed today—again, the life of the party, caring and so loving, and able to do so much for so many! I am so very, very thankful and just overwhelmed with unspeakable joy that Rachel did not lose or take her life but is living an abundant life with faith, love, and hope.

> The thief cometh not, but for to steal, and to kill, and to destroy: I am come that they might have life, and that they might have it more abundantly. (John 10:10)

Yes, our race can get hard and difficult, and at times, we slip, stumble, and fall for a righteous one falleth seven times (Proverbs 24:16). But God picks us up, heals our minds, our bodies, and our souls, and puts us back in the race saying, "Run on, run on for the race is not given to the swift nor the battle to the strong but to the one who endures to the end," (Ecclesiastes 9:11).

And soon and very soon ("Soon and Very Soon" by Andrae Crouch), we are back up to speed, "running by day and praying by night" ("I'm Not Tired Yet" by the Mississippi Mass Choir).

Well, it's the Lord's day, and we are in His house of prayer with tears rolling, hands lifted high and waving as we praise, worship, and thank God the Father, Jesus the Son, and the Holy Spirit! Praise God. Thank you, Jesus. Alleluia! For where would we be if it had not been for the Lord's grace, mercy, and miracles in our lives?

About the Authors

Keith Cooper is a product of many miracles. At seventy, he loves his marriage of forty-three years to Marlene. He enjoys playing with and teaching his grandchildren. He likes working with his wife. He also enjoys praying, writing, listening, giving, singing, and laughing. He tries to live in faith, staying positive, and full of hope. He loves walking, listening to music, gardening, and eating (mostly healthy stuff).

His favorite ministries were working in children's church, being a Sunday school teacher, and singing in various choirs.

Rachel C. Thomas, MEd, is a graduate of UCLA, a presidential appointee to the United States Advisory Council on Human Trafficking, and a personal survivor of human trafficking. She has extensive experience in teaching, training, curriculum writing, public speaking, and mentoring. As Executive Director of Sowers Education Group, she and a team work tirelessly to sow seeds of human trafficking awareness and survivor empowerment. Rachel has educated and inspired a wide range of audiences including teens, social service providers, churches, teachers, college students, and law enforcement. She is the lead author of the nation's most widely used sex trafficking intervention curriculum "Ending The Game" (*Journal Of Women and Criminal Justice*, 2021), as well as "The Cool Aunt Series" —, a human trafficking prevention course for teens. Since 2012, Rachel and the Sowers Team have reached over 150,000 live audience members and millions more through numerous media outlets including CNN, HLN, *The TD Jakes Show*, *The New York Times Upfront Magazine*, and ABC's *Newsmakers*. Rachel was honored by Congressman Ed Royce of California's thirty-ninth district and Los Angeles Supervisor, Don Knabe, for her leadership and trafficking prevention efforts (www.RachelCThomas.com).

Printed in the USA
CPSIA information can be obtained
at www.ICGtesting.com
LVHW022237090524
779584LV00004B/462

9 798890 437389